A Gift to:

From:

When God Is Silent

CHARLES R. SWINDOLL

COUNTRYMAN

Copyright © 2005 by Charles R. Swindoll, Inc.

Published by J. Countryman, a division of Thomas Nelson, Inc,
Nashville, Tennessee 37214.

Compiled and edited by Terri Gibbs

Unless otherwise indicated, all Scripture quotations in this book are from the
The New American Standard Bible (NASB) © 1960, 1962, 1963, 1971, 1972, 1973,
1975, 1977, and 1995 by the Lockman Foundation, and are used by permission.

Other Scripture references are from the following sources:

The New International Version of the Bible (NIV) © 1984 by the International
Bible Society. Used by permission of Zondervan Bible Publishers.

The Living Bible, (TLB) copyright © 1971. Used by permission of
Tyndale House Publishers, Inc., Wheaton, IL 60189. All rights reserved.

The Message (MSG), copyright © by Eugene H. Peterson, 1993, 1994, 1996.
Used by permission of NavPress Publishing Group.

Grateful acknowledgement is made for permission to use the material in this book, which originally
appeared in *Job: A Man of Heroic Endurance* published by the W Publishing Group, Nashville,
Tennessee, in 2004. The copyright to this material is held by Charles R. Swindoll, Inc.

Designed by LeftCoast Design, Portland, Oregon.

ISBN: 1-404101-470

Printed in the United States of America.

Contents

Preface

*J*ob was a man of unparalleled and genuine piety. He was also a man of well-deserved prosperity. He was a godly gentleman, extremely wealthy, a fine husband, and a faithful father. In a quick and brutal sweep of back-to-back calamities, Job was reduced to a twisted mass of brokenness and grief. The extraordinary accumulation of disasters that hit him would have been enough to finish off any one of us living today.

Job is left bankrupt, homeless, helpless, and childless. He's left standing beside the ten fresh graves of his now-dead children on a windswept hill. His wife is heaving deep sobs of grief as she kneels beside him, having just heard him say, "Whether our God gives to us or takes everything from us, we will follow Him." She leans over and secretly whispers, "Just

curse God and die." Pause and ponder their grief—and remember the man had done nothing to deserve such unbearable pain.

Misery and mystery are added to the insult and injury of Job's real-life disasters. As he sits there covered with skin ulcers that have begun erupting with pus, swelling his body with fever and giving him a maddening itch that will not cease, he looks up into the faces of three friends who arrive on the scene. They sit and stare at the man for seven days and nights without uttering a word. Just imagine. First, they don't recognize him, which tells you something of the extent of his swelling and the sores that covered his body. The sight causes them to be at a loss for words for a full week. Unfortunately, they didn't remain silent. When they finally did speak, they had nothing to say but blame, accusation, and insult. "You're getting what you deserve." Though they shaped their cutting remarks in much more philosophical terms, they proved unmerciful. His pain only intensified.

His misery turns to mystery with God's silence. If the words of his so-called friends are hard to hear, the silence of God becomes downright intolerable. Not until the thirty-eighth chapter of the book of *Job* does God finally break the silence, however long that took. If it were just a few months, try to imagine. You've become the object of your alleged friends' accusations, and the heavens are brass as you plead for answers from the Almighty, who remains mysteriously mute. Nothing comes to you by way of comfort. It's all so unfair; you've done nothing to deserve such anguish. So much for openers . . .

CHARLES R. SWINDOLL

Let's Start at the Beginning

The story begins with the remarkable résumé of a fine man. Job may become our hero of endurance, but let's remember he's only a man. He's not superman. He's not an angel in a human's body. He's just a man. "There was a man in the land of Uz, whose name was Job; and that man was blameless" (Job 1:1). It doesn't mean perfect; it means he did not compromise with moral evil. He was a man whose business dealings were handled with integrity. He kept his word. He dealt fairly with others. As a result, he was respected by those around him, whether within or outside the family. He was upright. He held God in respect, and he consistently eschewed evil. He was a man with character. And speaking of his family, Job was blessed with seven sons and three daughters. By the time Job's story gets told, all ten are grown. His was a life at its zenith.

By now he had amassed a remarkable number of possessions. Among them were 7,000 sheep. Much of the wool from the animals would have been sold. The portion held back could be woven into fabric that would be made into warm clothing for the cold winter days. The family's food would be provided from these animals and acres of crops. There were also 3,000 camels. I would imagine Job "ran a trucking business" for the caravans that went from east to west. No doubt, his camels were for hire. And those camels became his personal transportation. There were 1,000 oxen, yoked together in pairs to plow the fertile fields, preparing the soil for planting the seed that was later harvested for an abundance of food. And then we're told there were 500 female donkeys. In that ancient era, female donkeys provided the delicacy of the day—donkey milk.

Over and above all that was a happy, healthy family of ten adult children living nearby. No diapers to change. No baths to give. No carpools. No big meals to prepare. No lunches for school. No boys with big tattoos, driving sleek chariots, showing up and honking out front for the daughters. No teenaged daughters with nose rings and pierced belly buttons running around the house. All that's now behind Job and his wife. Job's got it made, and amazingly, no one was criticizing because there's nothing about him to criticize. Job had it made . . .

Suddenly there's a loud banging at the door of the big house. Once he opens that door, Job's life will never be the same. It's like the chilling phone call you would get in the middle of the night or the unexpected rap at your front door . . . an unannounced visit from someone wearing a uniform.

The messenger bursts in without being invited. He's winded and sobbing. With uncontrollable passion he blurts out, "The oxen . . . our oxen were plowing and the donkeys were feeding beside them, and the Sabeans . . . they attacked us! We've talked about the possibility of their coming; they've done it . . . they've assaulted us, master . . . and they took those animals, all the animals—and they've cut your servants to ribbons. I'm the only one who escaped!"

While he is still speaking, another messenger plunges into the scene. Without hesitation he screams: "There was this bolt of lightning, it was like fire that came down from heaven and in an instant it consumed all of the sheep and all of the field hands who take care of the sheep . . . and I'm the only one who made it out alive!"

Another pushes him aside as he grabs Job by his sleeve, "Master, you wouldn't believe it, but three raids from the Chaldeans have hit that area where we were preparing the camels for the next trip . . . they have taken all your camels away, and before leaving they murdered every one of your servants. I alone am left."

As Job stumbles to the side to regain his balance, surely he must have thought, "At least I've got my kids." Interrupting that thought, another workman plunges in, fighting back the tears. "Master Job, your sons and your daughters . . . they're all gone! There was this fierce tornado that swept through the wilderness, throwing wooden carts and animal carcasses into the air, and, Master, it kept coming with this deafening roar, it came right over the house of your oldest son, and the place exploded—and all of your children . . . were . . . killed."

Force yourself to pause and picture the scene. Just imagine . . .

When the Bottom
of Life Drops Out

W hen bad things happen, they often happen to the wrong person. And when that occurs, we're always left with that haunting word, "Why?"

That question is being asked in every major hospital around our nation today. Furthermore, every large community in every city has within it a home or two where that same question is still being asked without an answer.

Somewhere in all of this, there is room for the story of Job. For, as we have learned, a better man never lived in his day. He was not only a good man, he was a godly man. He was not only a faithful husband, he was a loving and devoted father. He was a good employer. His hard work and integrity had led to a prosperous lifestyle during the later years of his life. With plenty of land, an abundance of food, and sufficient livestock and camels to fund Job's dreams, it looked as though his entire future would be a downhill slide.

And then, the bottom of his life dropped out. Seemingly, senseless tragedy invaded the life of one who didn't deserve it. And he and his wife were left to pick up the pieces. He'd lost most of his servants, all but four. He'd lost all means of making a living. And he'd lost all ten of his grown children. To make matters worse, there was more to come. He had no idea that additional unfair and undeserved suffering lay ahead. Unexpected, it would level him. He dropped in bed the night before having no idea he'd never be the same in twenty-four hours.

Just like those workers in New York City on the tenth of September 2001. They left work late in the evening after a busy day in the World Trade Center already thinking about tomorrow. Putting their notes on their PDAs, they were making plans for the next day, completing their to-do list for 9/11. Many of them returned to their offices early the next morning to begin their work. A little before 8:00 a.m. they had no idea that American Airlines flight 11 was heading directly for their office in the

North Tower. Suddenly it struck. It was so surprising and unexpected, not even those in the South Tower knew of it and, for sure, had no idea that the terrorist plan was running its course for that tower, to be struck by United Flight 175 only eighteen minutes later. New Yorkers couldn't believe it—no one could believe it! It was beyond belief. Why them? Why that? Why now? Job's thoughts exactly, when all of his oxen and donkeys and camels and servants, and finally all ten of his children were gone. Seriously, what would have been your response?

Eugene Peterson gives us Job's response in the paraphrase of *The Message*.

> Job got to his feet, ripped his robe, shaved his head,
> then fell to the ground and worshiped:
> Naked I came from my mother's womb,
> naked I'll return to the womb of the earth.
> God gives, God takes.
> God's name be ever blessed.
> Not once through all this did Job sin;
> not once did he blame God.
>
> Job 1:20–22, MSG

Job fell to the ground. But, let's understand, this was not a collapse of grief, but for another purpose entirely. It is this that portrays the heroism of Job's endurance. He doesn't wallow and wail . . . he worships. The Hebrew verb means "to fall prostrate in utter submission and worship." I dare say most of us have never worshiped like that! I mean with your face on the ground, lying down, full-length. This was considered in ancient days the sincerest expression of obeisance and submission to the Creator-God.

By now, the only one cursing is Satan. He hated it! He resented Job's response! Of all things, the man still worships his God—the One who would allow these catastrophes to happen. There wouldn't be one in millions on this earth who would do so, but Job did exactly that. The wicked spirits sat with their mouths wide open as it were, as they watched a man who responded to all of his adversities with adoration; who concluded all of his woes with worship. No blame. No bitterness. No cursing. No clinched fist raised to the heavens screaming, "How dare you do this to me, after I've walked with you all these years!" None of that.

Instead, "Naked I came from my mother's womb, and naked I shall return there. Blessed be the Name of the LORD." That says it all. At birth we all arrived naked. At death we will all leave naked, as we're prepared for burial. We have nothing as we are birthed; we have nothing as we depart. So everything we have in between is provided for us by the Giver of Life. All we have is skin-wrapped bones, organs, nerves, and muscles, along with a soul for which we must give account before our God. Job has already taken care of that. It's as if he is saying, "The One who gave me life and has put everything on loan to me during my lifetime has chosen

(and has every right) to take everything away. I won't take anything with me anyway. Blessed be His name for loaning it to me while I had it. And blessed be His name for choosing to remove it."

Get that down nice and clearly. Get it, affluent Americans as we are. Get it when you stroll through your house and see all those wonderful belongings. Get it when you open the door and slip behind the steering wheel of your car. It's all on loan, every bit of it. Get it when the business falls and fails. It, too, was on loan. When the stocks rise, all that profit is on loan.

Face it squarely. You and I arrived in a tiny naked body (and not a great looking one at that!). And what will we have when we depart? A naked body plus a lot of wrinkles. You take nothing because you brought nothing! Which means you own nothing. What a grand revelation. Are you ready to accept it? You don't even own your children. They're God's children, on loan for you to take care of, rear, nurture, love, discipline, encourage, affirm, and then release.

This is a good place to consider a statement Paul wrote in his letter to his younger friend, Timothy. "For we have brought nothing into the world, so we cannot take anything out of it either. If we have food and covering, with these we shall be content" (1 Tim. 6:7–8). Put that not only in the margin of your Bible alongside Job 1:21, better still, tuck it in a permanent crease in your brain. We brought nothing in. We take nothing out. In the meantime, everything is on loan.

That explains how Job could say in all sincerity, "Blessed be the name of the LORD." And why the biblical narrative adds, "Through all this Job did not sin nor did he blame God" (Job 2:21–22). Since he never considered himself sole owner, Job had little struggle releasing the Lord's property. When you understand that everything you have is on loan, you are better prepared to release it when the owner wants it back.

We enter the world with our tiny fists clenched, screaming, but we always leave the world with hands open on our silent chests. Naked in, naked out. And in the interlude, "Lord God, blessed be Your name for loaning me everything I'm able to enjoy."

"Through all this Job did not sin." Isn't that wonderful? "Nor did he blame God." Why blame God? All things belong to Him. He is the sovereign owner of all. With 20/20 perspective, Job lifted himself off the ground, looked around at all that had changed, then put his arm around his grieving wife, held her close, and whispered, "God gave, and for some unrevealed reason, He chose to take back. He owns it all, sweetheart."

Accepting Adversity

"Then Satan went out from the presence of the LORD and smote Job with sore boils from the sole of his foot to the crown of his head" (Job 2:7). Job felt the sting of pain under his arm, and then he felt a swelling at his neck. Another couple of sores were inside his mouth. Small red spots appeared across his forehead, even up in his scalp. And of all things, his feet were so swollen he couldn't get his sandals on. Before noon his fever began to rage. By now he'd lost his appetite. It was like he was coming apart. He said something about it to his wife. She looked closer and noticed something like a rash breaking out. He asked her to check his back. She observed, "There are swollen marks all over." In the biblical account they are called "sore boils."

In addition, Job endured delirium, sleeplessness, and the rejection of friends (Job 7:3; 29:2). All of which lasted for months. In short, Job became the personification of misery.

We should remember that this resulted in Job's being rejected, isolated, and relocated to the city dump, as we would call it today. It was the place where they burned garbage and rubbish and human excrement from the city. That became his place of existence. Complete confusion, total isolation, unbearable pain, no hope of change, sitting in filthy surroundings, removed from all the comforts of home. In short, Job became "Ground Zero" in human form.

There came a day when all of this overwhelmed Mrs. Job. She could bear it no longer. At the end of her rope, she came to him for a visit. Sitting beside him, she leaned over and asked, "Do you still hold fast your integrity?" Quickly return to an earlier scene when God had said to Satan, "Have you noticed My servant Job? He still holds fast his integrity." Unknowingly she put her finger on the single quality in Job's life that God used in answering Satan. Her question called into question his need to maintain that any longer. And then she uses Satan's line when she says to her husband, "Curse God!" Satan was never closer to a smile than at that moment as he and his minions gathered near, staring, waiting, hoping. Surely they were urging, "Say it, Job. Say It! Go ahead—curse your God!" Everything hung on Job's response to his wife.

Job's response is magnificent. "You speak as one of the foolish women speaks" (Job 2:10). Hats off to the old patriarch! In his weakened condition, sitting there in the misery of all those sores, not knowing if any of that would ever change, he stood firm—he even reproved her. He said, in effect, "I need to correct the course of this conversation. We're not going there."

He went further than stating a reproof; he asked an excellent question. "Shall we indeed accept good from God and not accept adversity?" (Job 2:10). His insight was rare, not only back then, but today. What magnificent theology! How seldom such a statement emerges from our secular system.

Rather, we hear responses like, "What kind of a God is that who will treat you this unfairly after you have lived so devotedly? Why in the world would you continue to stand fast when this so-called loving God treats you like that?"

Job's counsel was different: "Shall we indeed accept good from God and not accept adversity?" The Hebrew sentence

reads, "The good shall we accept from God and the trouble shall we not accept?" emphasizing the good and the trouble. It's a rhetorical question, not asked to be answered but asked for the purpose of making the listener think it through. Job is thinking these thoughts: Doesn't He have the right? Isn't He the Potter? Aren't we the clay? Isn't He the

Shepherd and we the sheep? Isn't He the Master and we the servant? Isn't that the way it works?

Somehow he already knew that the clay does not ask the potter, "What are you making?" And so he says, in effect, "No, no, no, sweetheart. Let's not do that. We serve a God who has the right to do whatever He does and is never obligated to explain it or ask permission. Stop and consider—should we think that good things are all we receive? Is that the kind of God we serve? He's no heavenly servant of ours who waits for the snap of our fingers, is He? He is our Lord and our Master God! We need to remember that the God we serve has a game plan that is beyond our comprehension, hard times like this notwithstanding."

And I love this last line, "In all this Job did not sin with his lips"(v. 10). There's absolute trust there. And faith. "Sweetheart, we can't explain any of this, so let's wait and watch God work. We would never have expected what happened. Both our hearts are broken over the loss. We've lost everything. Well—not everything. We've still got each other. Our God has a plan that is unfolding even though we cannot understand it right now."

"BUT OUR GOD IS IN THE HEAVENS;
HE DOES WHATEVER HE PLEASES"

Psalm 115:3

Our God has no obligation to explain Himself. Our God does not have to step into a hospital room and say, "Now let me offer five reasons this has happened to your son." Understand, our God is full of compassion, but His plan is beyond our comprehension.

"For My thoughts are not your thoughts, neither are your ways My ways," declares the LORD. "For as the heavens are higher than the earth, so are My ways higher than your ways, and My thoughts than your thoughts" (Isaiah 55:8–9). And so we say, with Job: "O, God, I trust You. I don't know why I'm going through this. If there's something I can learn, wonderful. If there's something someone else can learn, great. Just get me through it. Just hold me close. Deepen me. Change me."

Job asked, "Shall we accept good from God and not accept adversity?" Because he knew that God is God, and someday He will make it clear. That's one of the reasons I believe heaven will be such a delightful place. When we step into His presence for the first time we will be given the panoramic view, and then (and not until then) we will respond, "So that's the reason! Now I get it!"

God is totally and completely and absolutely in charge. If He wipes out every member of your family, He is in charge. If He ends your business in abysmal bankruptcy, He is in charge. If the x-ray returns and it couldn't be worse, He is in charge. Please accept and submit to that teaching. How magnificent it is to find those who trust Him to the very end of this vale of suffering saying, "And may His name be praised. I don't understand it. Can't explain it. Nevertheless, may His name be praised." That is worship at its highest level.

May God enable us to raise our faith to such heights rather than lower our view of Him.

The Crucible

O ne day Job was a model of health and strength, a man of prosperity and integrity with a full quiver of children and happy, wholesome relationships with his circle of friends and workmen, only to lose it all in a matter of hours. Rather than reacting in panic and anger, the man heroically endures. In fact, since his day, Job has come to be known, not as the model of suffering but as the model of endurance.

I remind you of what is written of him in the middle of the first century, "You have heard of the endurance of Job" (James 5:11). Job endured the crucible; he didn't fight it or attempt to escape from it. The only ones he had left when all the dust settled was a wife and a small circle of friends from whom he received no affirmation. No encouragement. No comfort.

No soothing words of compassion. No embrace of affection. They only added stink to his stack. Nevertheless, Job endured.

A professor of history once said, "If Columbus had turned back, no one would have blamed him but nobody would have remembered him either." The single reason we remember Job with such admiration is because he endured.

Not only did he endure the afflictions I've described, he also endured the words of a grieving, shortsighted wife and the accusations of friends who took upon themselves the role of judge and jury. If you have gone through your own crucible, chances are good you know what it is like in the midst of pain to have people turn against you. What pain that brings! But, returning to the definition, that's when the crucible causes change and development. As a result of enduring pain, we change from being mere sufferers to wise counselors and valuable comforters.

The most valuable counsel I have received in my life has never come from a novice. It's come from those who bore the scars of the crucible.

When God Is Silent

We need to understand that God's "wonderful plan" for our lives is wonderful from His perspective, not yours and mine. To us, "wonderful" means comfortable, healthy, all bills paid, no debt, never sick, happily married with two well-behaved children, a fulfilling, well-paying job, and the anticipation of nothing but blessing and success and prosperity forever. That's "wonderful" to us. But God's wonderful plan is not like that.

Job brings us back to reality—God's kind of reality. Remember his question, the one he asked his wife? "Shall we accept good from God and not accept adversity?" And remember that closing line? "In all this Job did not sin with his lips" (Job 2:10).

The same man soon steps into a whole new frame of reference.

LET THE DAY PERISH ON WHICH I WAS TO BE BORN,
AND THE NIGHT WHICH SAID, "A BOY IS CONCEIVED."

Job 3:3

WHY DID I NOT DIE AT BIRTH,
COME FORTH FROM THE WOMB AND EXPIRE?

Job 3:11

Job's responses here make us uneasy. We don't want our hero to think or talk like he does. He doesn't seem like he's a man of God anymore. He has the audacity to say, "I am not at ease. I am not quiet. I am not at rest. I am in turmoil." What has happened? We are given entrance into a dark side of Job's life that is as real as any of our lives today, but the difference is, Job lets it all out. Thankfully, he reminds us that even the godly can be depressed.

Job's outburst is not mainly due to his physical suffering. It's more emotional—prompted by his losing touch with God. His grief and bankruptcy and painful sores don't cause him to say what he says in Job 3. Obviously, his pain plays a role in it, but that's not the underlying cause. It isn't because he can't sleep at night. These are not nocturnal meanderings that come because

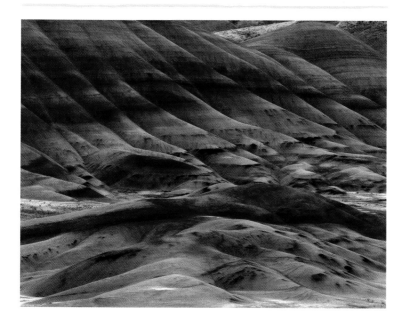

he's restless. He is at the bottom of his emotional barrel because he's lost his best Friend. For many years God seemed intimate. As his business grew and the camel caravans multiplied, and bumper crops were harvested and the profit began to pour in, blessing him and his family with enormous prosperity, he and God remained on close speaking terms. They walked hand in hand . . . until that awful day when everything broke loose. As we've seen, he lost everything—all of the animals, their home, all ten adult children, and finally, his health. That was terrible, but this isn't what depressed him.

His real darkness came when the heavens became brass. When God no longer walked with him in the cool of the evening. When God no longer spoke to him and reassured him with words like, "My son, let me explain what this is all about. Satan came and he dared Me to do this, claiming that you would curse Me. I knew you'd never do that. Furthermore, I want you to know, I'm right here with you through all of this." Job knew none of that. Matter of fact, he knew nothing of the *why*, only *what*. He's just living in the consequences of those horrific events. And worst of all, God is silent, and He seems absent.

The man has now reached the end of his rope. You've been there. This is the day you slam the door shut. This is the day you say to those close to you, "Leave me alone!" This is the day in his life when he cannot find his Friend.

I don't know that I would have been mature enough earlier in my life to do this, but today, as I think of hearing Job who is so crushed, with his head in his hands and probably dissolved in tears, I could not restrain myself from walking over to him, putting my arms around him, and telling him how much I love him and respect him. Though admittedly, I'm sure I could never understand how terrible his misery must be.

Having said all that, there are three practical statements I want to give you who can identify with Job's struggle:

First, *there are days too dark for the sufferer to see light.*

Second, *there are experiences too extreme for the hurting to have hope.* When a person drops so low due to the inner pain, it's as if all hope is lost. That's why Job admits his lack of ease, his absence of peace, and his deep unrest.

Third, *there are valleys too deep for the anguished to find relief.* It seems, at that point, there is no reason to go on.

We run out of places to look to find relief. It's then our minds play tricks on us, making us think that not even God cares. Wrong! Do you remember the line that Corrie ten Boom used to quote? I often call it to mind: "There is no pit so deep but that God is not deeper still." I know, I know. Those who are deeply depressed don't remember that and can't reason with that. They would deny such a statement because they feel a

vast distance between them and God, and it's confusing—it's frightening. But the good news is that God is not only there . . . He cares.

I think it is noteworthy that God doesn't respond to Job's confusion by saying, "Shame on you, Job." God could handle Job's words. He understood why he said what he said. And He understands you. Unfortunately, Job has his words on record for preachers to talk about for centuries. Yours and mine, thankfully, will remain a secret inside our cars, or in the back part of our bedrooms, or along the crashing surf, or perhaps out under tall trees in a forest. God can handle it all, so let it all out. Tell Him all that's in your heart. You never get over grief completely until you express it fully. Don't hold back.

It's Okay to Say: "I don't know"

Here is an important lesson for us to learn from Job: *There are times when God's ways only make us more confused.* My point? Don't expect to understand everything that happens when it occurs.

I'm going to offer a simple suggestion that may make you smile. It's something I want you to practice in front of a mirror. I call it, "The Shrug." Stare into the mirror, shake your head and shrug your shoulders, then say out loud, "I don't know." Practice that little maneuver several times a month.

I don't care if you have a Ph.D. you earned at Yale or in Scotland. Just stand in front of the mirror, all alone, nobody around, shrug, and say, "I don't know . . . I really don't know." You can add, "I can't tell you why that happened. I don't know." Repeat the words several times: "I don't know."

The great news is that God never shrugs. He never says that. With acute perception He says, "I know exactly why this happened. I know the way you take. I know why. I know how long you'll be there, and I know what will be the end result." Shrugging and deity are incompatible.

While you're shrugging in genuine humility, saying, "I don't know," He's saying, "Good for you. Rely on Me in the mystery. Trust Me." God never promised He would inform us ahead of time all about His plan, He's just promised He has one. Ultimately, it's for our good and His glory. He knows—we don't. That's why we shrug and admit, "I don't know." So, if you and I meet someday and you ask me a deep, difficult question, don't be surprised if I shrug and say, "I don't know."

But I do know this: The death of His Son was not in vain. And I do know this: Christ died for you. And I do know this: If you believe in Him, He will forgive your sins and you will go to live with Him forever. You'll have heaven and all the blessings of it, I do know that. It's a tough journey, getting there. Full of a lot of confusion, a lot of struggle, a lot of shrugs, followed by a lot of "I don't knows." But when the heavens open and we're there, hey, there will be no more shrugs. "Now I know."

When Hope Goes Missing

When we were at Dallas Theological Seminary, Cynthia and I lived in the old Campus Apartments. But back in our day, we lived in Campus Apartment number nine (almost sounds like a prison cell, doesn't it?). I'm telling you, we had roaches. I said to Cynthia one evening, "We don't have a single roach in our place." She stared at me like I was absolutely nuts. I said, "Actually, they're all married and have large families!" Problems are like that.

Job was distressed over God's apparent absence and very obvious silence. That may sound shocking to some who read those words, but it happens, especially among those who are hurting.

MY SPIRIT IS BROKEN,

MY DAYS USED UP,

MY GRAVE DUG AND WAITING.

Job 16:7–17:1, MSG

Those are strong, deeply emotional words from a distressed man.

Remember, Job still doesn't know the arrangement between Satan and God. He still doesn't know why one day, completely out of the blue, the bottom drops out, bringing tornadoes and fires, destruction and multiple deaths . . . finally ill health with such force. Not once does God give him a word of explanation. Remember, all of his adult life Job has walked intimately with God. He has been obedient and submissive—now this! No wonder he's distressed.

I'll confess to you, I've known that kind of confusion—but certainly not like Job. During such times, I have said in unguarded moments, "God what in the world are You up to? What is this about? To the best of my knowledge, I am not doing anything wrong. And I'm not doing it with the wrong motive. I haven't gone into this to please myself or to impress

somebody else. I'm trying to walk in obedience. But everything has backfired! What's going on, Lord?"

It's like driving home from work after a terrible day at the office. In bumper-to-bumper traffic, the guy behind you smashes into you. You then hit the car in front of you, and it happens to be a new Porsche. Porsche drivers tend not to like that when you hit them from the rear. You get everything documented by the police. And the Porsche owner is so angry he threatens to sue you. And when you finally do get home, you don't have any

milk. Your dog's hungry and he's been gnawing on the cabinet. Your kids are mean, so they're gnawing on each other. And the mail is full of overdue bills, and you're out of money. And your wife tells you she got the results of the biopsy . . . and the doc wants both of you to come see him first thing in the morning. That does it! You think, "What is this all about, God? And while I'm at it, where are You?"

And no answer comes . . . and tomorrow is worse than today. And next week is intensifying all of it, making last week look like a downhill slide. On top of all of that, you are about to lose your job. And the guy in the Porsche *does* sue you. And. And. And. And.

In unguarded moments when the lights are out and the doors are closed, and your pastor isn't around to listen, and nobody's going to tell on you, you do slump and start wondering. If you don't you're weird. Don't tell me you're too spiritual to think like that. Like Job, your spirit is broken, your days leave you exhausted and confused, and it's like your grave is dug and awaiting your arrival. The result? *Again, he is depressed.* And how could anyone be surprised?

What, specifically, brought Job to this point of depression? I believe it's best expressed in the Latin words, *Deus absconditus*. I came across those words this week. . . . *Deus* is the Latin word for God. *Absconditus* gives us our English word abscond. Webster says it means "to conceal, to depart secretly and hide oneself." God has secretly split the scene. That's it, exactly!

"He's gone. I can't figure Him out. When I pray I don't get answers. When I devote myself even more deeply to doing His will for all the right reasons, I continue to lose. When I pray, zip happens. God has *absconded* with the blessings."

> MY LIFE'S ABOUT OVER. ALL MY PLANS ARE SMASHED,
> ALL MY HOPES ARE SNUFFED OUT—
> MY HOPE THAT NIGHT WOULD TURN INTO DAY,
> MY HOPE THAT DAWN WAS ABOUT TO BREAK.
>
> Job 17:11–12, MSG

The kind of faith God values seems to develop best when everything fuzzes over, when God stays silent, when the fog rolls in.

PHILLIP YANCEY

Disgusted

Distressed

Depressed

Despondent

Job has reached absolute rock bottom. Death seems his only recourse, the one refuge of relief. Right now, the grave seems mighty inviting.

You know what he's missing? He is missing what only grace can bring him. *Hope.* He has no grace from anybody around him, so he's left with no hope. Nobody there to reassure him. He is totally confused. He can't find his way.

You know why I love the Bible? Because it's *so* real. There's a lot of fog rolling into Job's life just like in our lives. On this earth nobody "lives happily ever after." That line is a huge fairy tale. You're living in a dream world if you're waiting for things to get "happy ever after." That's why we need grace. Marriage doesn't get easier, it gets harder. So we need grace to keep it together. Work doesn't get easier, it gets more complicated, so we need grace to stay on the job. Childrearing doesn't get easier. You who have babies one, two, three years old—you think you've got it tough. Wait until they're fourteen. Or eighteen. Talk about needing grace!

Everything gets harder. You thought you were fat when you got married. Take a glance in the mirror this evening. That's why I often tell brides and grooms, "Enjoy the wedding pictures; you'll never be *thinner*." That's tough to face, but it's the truth. So? We need *grace* as we gain weight! We need *grace* to go on! Grace and more grace—*God's grace*. We need *grace* to relate to

each other. We need *grace* to drive. We need *grace* to stay positive.
We need *grace* to keep a church in unity. We need *grace* to be
good neighbors. We really need *grace* as we get older.

I'll be painfully honest here. If I called the shots, I would
have relieved Job five minutes after he lost everything. I'd have
brought all his kids back to life the very next day. I would have
immediately re-created everything he lost, and I would really deal
with those sorry comforters! I'd have cut the lips off of Eliphaz
after about three sentences. And if that didn't shut him up, I'd
take the neck. I mean . . . who needs that clod? But you know
what? You would never mature under my kind of treatment.
You'd just enjoy the comfort. We'd all go to picnics then on a
motorcycle ride and have tons of fun. That's my style. Which
explains why Cynthia says to me, "Honey, if everybody handled
things like you wanted, all we'd bring to the party is *balloons*.
Nobody would think to bring the food." As usual, she's right.

So, the fog's rolled in. As all hell breaks loose, grace takes a
hike. Welcome to the human race, Job.

Leave Room for Mystery

*H*ere's another message that Job teaches us. *We must leave room for mystery.* The theology of some folks doesn't have room for mystery. Everything is black or white. If you obey, you will be blessed. Those in God's will enjoy great prosperity and good health. But if you suffer, you're *out* of God's will. He wants *everybody* well. What flawed theology! Since God is sovereign and all powerful, if He wanted everybody well, we'd all be well. After all, He's God . . . but it's not like that.

He's running the show, if you will. He deliberately allows sickness. For mysterious reasons beyond our comprehension, He permits pain. And then there are other times for reasons that are clearly revealed, He tests us. The point is, He is in charge. That means we're not. (I'm sounding like Yogi Berra.) If we pray for the healing of an individual, and healing doesn't occur, we are not to conclude it's his or her fault. Because *God doesn't want everyone well*. Please read that sentence again.

Paul prayed three separate times that his thorn in the flesh would be taken from him. And the Lord answered "No, no, no." Paul not only stopped praying for relief, he accepted God's firm no as final. Then he responded with an acceptance speech that cannot be improved on:

> HE HAS SAID TO ME, "MY GRACE IS SUFFICIENT FOR YOU, FOR POWER IS PERFECTED IN WEAKNESS." MOST GLADLY, THEREFORE, I WILL RATHER BOAST ABOUT MY WEAKNESSES, SO THAT THE POWER OF CHRIST MAY DWELL IN ME. THEREFORE I AM WELL CONTENT WITH WEAKNESSES, WITH INSULTS, WITH DISTRESSES, WITH PERSECUTIONS, WITH DIFFICULTIES, FOR CHRIST'S SAKE; FOR WHEN I AM WEAK, THEN I AM STRONG.
>
> 2 Corinthians 12:9–10

What a magnificent, mature response! Paul was willing to accept the mystery of God's will in leaving him with the affliction after he had urgently prayed for relief three times!

The major message Job leaves us is fairly obvious by now: Even though God is elusive and mysterious, strange and silent, invisible and seemingly passive, *He is trustworthy*. In light of that, I want to suggest these three lessons that linger.

First, resist the temptation to explain everything; *God knows*.

Second, focus on the future benefits, not the present pain; *God leads*.

Third, embrace the sovereignty of the Almighty; *God controls*.

Refuse to believe that life is based on blind fate or random chance. Everything that happens, including the things you cannot explain or justify, is being woven together like an enormous, beautiful piece of tapestry. From this earthly side it seems blurred and knotted, strange and twisted. But from heaven's perspective it has an incredible pattern. Best of all, it is for God's greater glory. Right now, it seems so confusing, but someday the details will come together and make good sense.

We Cannot Explain
the Inexplicable

*A*ll the way through Job's story, it is God who captures our attention and makes us wonder. He confuses us.

We who were reared in the church learned from our earliest years that God is good, loving, merciful, compassionate, just, fair, holy, full of mercy and grace. He "sympathizes with our weaknesses" (Hebrews 4:15), "knows what you need before you ask Him" (Matthew 6:8), and "satisfies your years with good things" (Psalm 103:5). Remember the memorized mealtime prayer? "God is great, God is good, let us thank Him for this food. Amen."

Then we encounter Job. And we see God stepping back into the shadows, permitting Satan to afflict His godly servant, as He stays silent, keeps a distance, and refuses to answer when Job pleads for an explanation. I'll go ahead and say it—all that seems downright cruel. If not cruel, it is certainly in conflict with the God we met as kids in Sunday school.

And so we're left with one of two conclusions. Either we weren't given a complete and correct understanding of our God, or we do not really understand the story of Job. I suggest it's the former. The picture we were given in Sunday school was incomplete.

Paul wrote a brief yet profound statement regarding the Lord our God in Romans 11:33. I ask you to pause and let its words sink in. Read it slowly, preferably aloud, and read it more than once before going on.

> OH, THE DEPTH OF THE RICHES BOTH OF THE WISDOM
> AND KNOWLEDGE OF GOD! HOW UNSEARCHABLE ARE
> HIS JUDGMENTS AND UNFATHOMABLE HIS WAYS!

Please take the time to ponder two words in that second sentence. *Unsearchable. Unfathomable.* Allow them to land with full weight on your mind.

As far back as the first century, when Paul penned his letter, he informed his readers in Rome (ultimately us), that God is *unfathomable* and *unsearchable*. Now, don't misunderstand. That doesn't mean He stops being good, and it doesn't mean He is no longer loving and merciful. He is  still all of that but so much more. He is also incomprehensible.

He is deep. His ways are beyond our understanding, seeming mysterious and inexplicable to us. The longer we think on this the more we realize there is a lot about God we were never taught. In the midst of our study of Job, we are forced to dig much deeper into His character and discover new depths. In a word, God is *inscrutable*.

One of the first times I remember that word making a dent in my brain occurred when I was graduating from seminary in the spring of 1963. The president of Dallas Seminary was the late Dr. John F. Walvoord, a man I always admired for his clear-thinking, theological mind. He told our graduating class that he hoped all of us would continue to remember that our God is inscrutable. He then quoted Romans 11:33. Looking around the campus chapel audience, he added with a wry smile, "There will be times you will try to unscrew the inscrutable. You cannot do so!" As usual, Dr. Walvoord was right. But we so want to do that. Everything within us longs to explain everything about God and interpret all His ways and come to a full understanding of all His workings.

After all, God made us intelligent beings. Furthermore, He instructs us to know Him. Longing to do that, we continue to pursue this divine understanding, but the deeper we dig, the more unfathomable He becomes. Why, of course! That shouldn't surprise us, but we're frustrated not knowing. We prefer things fathomable, or, if you will, "scrutable." We want to be able to explain and correctly analyze *whatever*, so that we understand the whole story. But that is impossible when it comes to the living and reigning God.

It is especially important that we realize He is not like us, neither are His methods like ours. Not even a little bit. As the prophet Isaiah reminds us of God:

> "For My thoughts are not your thoughts,
> Neither are your ways My ways," declares the Lord
> "For as the heavens are higher than the earth,
> So are My ways higher than your ways
> And My thoughts than your thoughts."
>
> Isaiah 55:8–9

We are finite; He is infinite. Our ways are limited; His unlimited. We are small; He is vast.

God Does All Things Well

May I tell you something that may make you uncomfortable? God doesn't have a "wonderful plan" for everybody's life. Not here on earth, for sure. For some lives His plan is Lou Gehrig's disease. For some lives (like Job's) His plan is a life of pain. For others, heartbreak and brokenness, blindness or paralysis, or congenital complications. For many, His plan is No to their requests for healing. But we don't like that. Some won't accept that. In fact, they go so far as to say, "If you believe that, you lack faith." On the contrary, if you believe that, you believe the Bible!

The God of the Bible includes the lives of people who do not get well, who do not quickly get over their problems, who do not easily overcome accidents or illnesses. God's Word pictures its heroes, warts and all. They hurt. They fall. They fail, and on occasion, by His grace, they succeed.

BEHOLD, THESE ARE THE FRINGES OF HIS WAYS;
AND HOW FAINT A WORD WE HEAR OF HIM!
BUT HIS MIGHTY THUNDER, WHO CAN UNDERSTAND?

Job 26:14

Isn't that a thrilling thought? Isn't that a great word? The fringes, the outer edges of His ways; only the quiet whispers of His mighty voice, the hushed tones of omnipotence! And to think that this Creator-God pierces through all the millions of galaxies of "the heavens" and gives His attention to this tiny green-pea planet called Earth, reaching down to folks like us, knowing even the hairs on our head. David was right: "It is too high, I cannot attain to it."

WHAT IS MAN THAT YOU TAKE THOUGHT OF HIM,
AND THE SON OF MAN THAT YOU CARE FOR HIM?

Psalm 8:4

Indeed, how unsearchable are His judgments and unfathomable are His ways. Now, be careful here. That does not mean He's not in touch, out of control, and He doesn't have a plan. It just means He isn't obligated to explain Himself. And because He doesn't reveal everything, we're left with three very honest words, which are helpful coming from the lips of otherwise proud people.

And what are those three words? *I don't know.*

In the final analysis, God knows, and He does all things well. He is in charge. I am the clay; He is the Potter. I am the disciple; He is the Lord. I am the sheep; He is the Shepherd. I am the servant; He is the Master. That means I am to submit myself. I am to humble myself under His mighty hand. I must be willing to adjust my life to His choices for me, to listen, to learn, to adapt to His leading wherever it may go whether I'm comfortable, happy, or healthy. That is obedience. Job by now is beginning to see it, and when he reaches the end of his brief explanation, he wisely asks, "Who can understand?"

Train yourself to think theologically. Make it your determined purpose to think God's thoughts after Him, acknowledging His lofty magnificence. Teach yourself to be at ease saying the words, "I don't know."

Because Job thought correctly about God, he was able to endure, even while not understanding why. May his tribe increase.

Understanding What
Really Matters

⁓

Each time our nation returns to another anniversary of September 11, we pause and reflect on all that happened: The synchronized, premeditated strategy of multiple murders that shocked us; the headlines and pictures that filled our news papers and magazines for weeks; the thousands of families who grieved the loss of loved ones. Each year we read the testimonies of real people who were devastated by that series of atrocities. It isn't uncommon for them to include words that mention some of the lessons learned, resulting in renewed commitments to priorities.

One surviving New York cop said, "As a result of those atrocities, I will never again take our liberty for granted."

A middle-aged widow, whose husband was killed in the World Trade Center, expressed it this way, "I now hug my children tightly every day. I always tell them I love them every morning and every evening before we go to bed." One forty-eight-year-old stockbroker who lost several coworkers on 9/11 admitted, "I've decided to hold my business and my career much more loosely; my family and friends have now become more important to me." Suffering helps clear away the fog that success and prosperity create.

I have finally come to realize that one of the benefits of going through times of suffering is that my focus turns vertical. Charles Spurgeon, the great pulpiteer of London for so many years, was a flashpoint of controversy. The media of his day relished taking him on. They took advantage of a target that big. Normally he could hold his own, but there was one occasion when it began to get the best of him. All of us have our breaking point.

His wife noticed a depression that was lingering. She became concerned for him that he not lose his zeal and not miss the opportunities that were his while going through such hard times. That led her to do an unusual thing. She turned in her Bible to the Sermon on the Mount where Jesus said:

Blessed are you when people insult you and persecute you, and falsely say all kinds of evil against you because of me. Rejoice and be glad, for your reward in heaven is great; for in the same way they persecuted the prophets who were before you.

Matthew 5:11–12

In her own handwriting she wrote those words on a large piece of paper. She then taped it on the ceiling above their bed. When the preacher turned over the next morning, he awoke, blinked his eyes, and as he lay there he read those words. He read them again, aloud. He focused vertically on what God was saying, and it renewed him within. He pressed on with new passion. What a wonderful, creative idea Mrs. Spurgeon had!

When flat on our backs, the only way to look is up. It worked. He stopped licking his wounds. He looked past all the criticism and began again to be preoccupied with thoughts of God.

Thinking God's thoughts is our highest goal. I call it thinking theologically or thinking biblically. That is one of the reasons I'm such a proponent of the discipline of Scripture memorization. You cannot think God's thoughts more acutely than when you quote God's very words back to life's situations.

What comes into our minds when we think about God is the most important thing about us. And so what comes to mind when *you* think about God? I remember as a little boy thinking of God as a very old man with a long white beard, cheeks puffed out, blowing strong winds from the north. I had seen His face at school on old maps of the world.

What comes to your mind when you think about God? Do you see Him as the One who gives you breath and keeps your heart beating? Do you see Him as the One who will call everyone into judgment someday? Do you see Him as the One who watches over your children and your business? Do you acknowledge His power is greater than any power you would ever witness on this earth? Or, honestly now, is He a little remote, sort of out of touch with today's hi-tech society? Your view of God makes all the difference in how you view life.

Suffering enabled Job to grasp deep truths. In fact, he moved from the realm of mere knowledge or intellectual information to wisdom or spiritual perception.

BUT WHERE CAN WISDOM BE FOUND?

AND WHERE IS THE PLACE OF UNDERSTANDING?

MAN DOES NOT KNOW ITS VALUE,

NOR IS IT FOUND IN THE LAND OF THE LIVING.

THE DEEP SAYS, "IT IS NOT WITH ME."

AND THE SEA SAYS, "IT IS NOT WITH ME."

PURE GOLD CANNOT BE GIVEN IN EXCHANGE FOR IT,

NOR CAN SILVER BE WEIGHED AS ITS PRICE.

Job 28:12–15

Consider what Job's saying, "Dig into the earth, you'll find precious jewels and metals, but you won't find wisdom. Probe into the outer spaces and the mysteries will unfold, but you'll not find wisdom. Study nature's wonders, examine all that this earth holds for you, and there will be exciting discoveries, but *you won't find wisdom!"*

This assures us that as helpful as an education may be, reading widely or traveling broadly, or even being mentored by the brightest, none of that will automatically result in wisdom. It is not found in textbooks. Or discoveries. Or inventions. Or in some guru's mind.

Allow me to offer a simple definition of *wisdom*. Wisdom is looking at life from God's point of view. When we employ wisdom we are viewing life as God sees it. That's why it's so valuable to think God's thoughts after Him. You look at difficulties and tests as God looks at them. You look at family life and child rearing as God looks at them. You interpret current events as God would interpret them. You focus on the long view. You see the truth even though all around you are deception and lies.

Let's go a step further and define another scriptural term: *understanding.* What does it mean? Understanding is responding to life's struggles and challenges as God would have us respond. Not in panic and confusion. Not forfeiting those things that are valuable to us, and not by compromising our integrity. Instead, when we have understanding, we respond to life's challenges as God would have us respond. We trust Him. We believe in Him. We refuse to be afraid. We don't operate our lives according to human impulses or in step with today's politically correct culture.

How terribly important it is that we stand firm in wisdom, responding in understanding. Neither can be found by our own effort or as a result of our searching. Then where does this *wisdom* come from? Where can we find true *understanding*?

GOD UNDERSTANDS ITS WAY,
AND HE KNOWS ITS PLACE.
AND TO MAN HE SAID "BEHOLD THE FEAR OF THE LORD,
THAT IS WISDOM;
AND TO DEPART FROM EVIL IS UNDERSTANDING."

Job 28:23 & 28

You can earn four Ph.D. degrees and never get wisdom or understanding. You'll certainly not get a grasp of the fear of the Lord from higher learning. Even in the finest of universities, there's no course offered on the fear of the Lord. The source? God and God alone. By "fear of the Lord" I'm referring to an awesome respect for God accompanied by a personal hatred for sin. Now we can see why Solomon wrote, "The fear of the LORD is the beginning of wisdom, and the knowledge of the Holy One is understanding" (Proverbs 9:10).

God Governs Justly

G od is sovereign. He is not only good all the time, He is in *control* all the time. "Even when I'm sick?" Yes, even when you are sick. "Even when I can't understand why?" Yes, even when you can't explain the reasons. "Like this right now?" you ask. Absolutely. God is never shocked or surprised. Our lives, therefore, are never out of God's control. And furthermore, God doesn't feel obligated to explain Himself. The truth is, even if He did, most of us still wouldn't get it, because His ways are deep and His plan is profound. In hopes of driving this significant truth home, I will repeat it: God is sovereign, and He doesn't explain Himself, nor should He feel obligated to do so.

> GOD THUNDERS WITH HIS VOICE WONDROUSLY,
> DOING GREAT THINGS WHICH WE CANNOT COMPREHEND.

Job 37:1–5

God is prominent and preeminent. He is majestic in His power, magnificent in His person, and marvelous in His purposes. How refreshing to step back in the shadows of our own insignificance and give full attention to the greatness of our God! *It's all about Him!*

How unlike the little girl walking beside her mother in a pouring rain and loud thunderstorm. Every time the lightning flashed, her mother noticed she turned and smiled. They'd walk a little further, then lightning, and she'd turn and smile. The mother finally said, "Sweetheart, what's going on? Why do you always turn and smile after the flash of lightning?" "Well," she said, "Since God is taking my picture, I want to be sure and smile for Him."

We take a major step toward maturity when we finally realize it's not about us and our significance. It is all about God's magnificence. His holiness. His greatness. His glory.

> THE LORD IS GOOD,
> A STRONGHOLD IN THE DAY OF TROUBLE,
> AND HE KNOWS THOSE WHO TAKE REFUGE IN HIM.
>
> Nahum 1:7

God is transcendent. He is magnificent. He is mighty. He alone is awesome! He is all around us, above us, and within us. Without Him there is no righteousness. Without Him there is no holiness. Without Him there is no promise of forgiveness, no source of absolute truth, no reason to endure, no hope beyond the grave.

> *AROUND GOD IS AWESOME MAJESTY.*
> *THE ALMIGHTY—WE CANNOT FIND HIM;*
> *HE IS EXALTED IN POWER*
> *AND HE WILL NOT DO VIOLENCE TO JUSTICE*
> *AND ABUNDANT RIGHTEOUSNESS.*
> *THEREFORE MEN FEAR HIM;*
> *HE DOES NOT REGARD ANY WHO ARE WISE OF HEART.*
>
> Job 37:22–24

Nothing compares to Him. Let us never forget that! Let us worship Him and bow down before Him and exalt His name in words, in silence, and in song.

How big is your God? Big enough to intervene? Big enough to be trusted? Big enough to be held in awe and ultimate respect? Big enough to erase your worries and replace them with peace?

When your God is too small, your problems are magnified and you retreat in fear and insecurity. When your God is great, your problems pale into insignificance and you stand in awe as you worship the King.

The Silence Is Broken

When God broke the silence, he bolted forth "out of the whirlwind" (Job 38:1). All of us who have waited and ached so long with Job to hear God's voice, we now say with a sigh, "Finally!"

Once God breaks the silence, He gives two "speeches." His first message is recorded in Job 38:1–40:5. His second begins at Job 40:6. I find it interesting and surprising what God does *not* do. He doesn't give Job any *answers* to his questions. He doesn't *apologize* for having been silent so long. He doesn't offer a hint of information about the whole thing between Himself and Satan way back when it all started. Furthermore, God doesn't *acknowledge* that Job has been through deep struggles. When He finally speaks, He begins with a reproof.

That is not meant to be cruel, only to stop Job in his tracks. He needs a refresher course on who's in charge. He needs to realize that God's ways and works are beyond his ability to understand. He needs to realize just how many things are beyond his comprehension. So God turns to the vast dimensions of His creative work. Read slowly and try to imagine God's lecture:

> HAVE YOU ENTERED INTO THE SPRINGS OF THE SEA
> OR WALKED IN THE RECESSES OF THE DEEP?
> TELL ME, IF YOU KNOW ALL THIS.
> WHERE IS THE WAY TO THE DWELLING OF LIGHT?
> AND DARKNESS, WHERE IS ITS PLACE,
> THAT YOU MAY TAKE IT TO ITS TERRITORY
> AND THAT YOU MAY DISCERN THE PATHS TO ITS HOME?
>
> Job 38:16–20

In my research I found that the deepest place in all the oceans has been discovered to be 6.78 miles. There may be deeper places, but that's as deep as has been determined as of today—a little over six-and-three-quarter miles beneath the surface.

And the expanse of the stellar spaces? You may remember it took one of our space probes twelve years to cover 4.4 billion miles,

ultimately passing within 3,000 miles of Neptune's cloudbank.
But that represents space travel only in our *immediate* galaxy.
I'm told there are hundreds of thousands, maybe millions more.
And who knows but what ours is the smallest of all those in
space? It's mind-boggling. Especially when you consider that the
One who could answer every question is asking the questions.
He not only created it, He set it all in motion and keeps
everything moving in clockwork precision.

How did Job respond? He responded with humility, relief, and surrender. That's all God wanted to hear.

Job's response prompts me to think of what this says to our twenty-first-century world. What needed messages it offers to our times! I find at least three of them between the lines of Job's response.

The first: *If God's ways are higher than mine, then whatever He allows I bow before Him in submission.* The result of that attitude is *true humility.* Submission to the Father's will is the mark of genuine humility. And all of us could use a huge dose of that. How unusual to find a humble spirit in our day, especially among the competent, the highly intelligent, the successful.

Here's the second: *If God is in full control, then however He directs my steps, I follow in obedience.* What *relief* that brings! Finally—I can relax, since I'm not in charge.

Here's the third: *If God has answers I lack, then whenever He speaks, I listen in silence.* In the process of listening, I learn. Learning requires our slowing down, patiently waiting for God to work, staying ready to listen as He instructs us in His ways.

Do you know what Job finally realized? It is all about God, not me. Job got it! And what does that mean?

- God's purpose is unfolding and I cannot hinder it.

- God's plan is incredible and I will not comprehend it.

- God's reproof is reliable and I dare not ignore it.

- God's way is best and I must not resist it.

Have you learned those things yet? Have you come to realize your business is about your God. Your family is about your God. Everything you claim to possess, He owns. Every privilege you enjoy is granted by His grace. None of it is deserved. Job got all that . . . the question is, have you? Tragically, many don't get it until faced with impossible moments.

How satisfying a submissive life can be. The blend is beautiful to behold: a strong-hearted person, who is surrendered and humbled with a "broken and contrite spirit"—entertaining no grudges, making no demands, having no expectations, offering no conditions, anticipating no favors, fully repentant before the Lord God. And the marvelous result? The Lord begins to use us in amazing ways. Why? Because the world doesn't see that unique combination very often.

Take Hope

*B*ack when his body was covered with sores, back when his friends were still against him, when he was still bankrupt sitting in a garbage dump at the outskirts of the city, Job had the temerity to say, "But He knows the way I take; when He has tried me, I shall come forth as gold" (Job 23:10).

Look at that one more time. The H is capitalized since the pronoun is referring to the living God. Job makes three statements based on faith in the midst of his suffering. All three are about his God.

First: I know that God knows my situation. "He knows the way I take."

Second: I believe it is God who is testing me. "When He has tried me."

Third: I believe that after the trials have ended, He will bless me in a unique way. In fact, I will emerge a better man. There will be goldlike blessings that will emerge following this affliction. Quite a remarkable statement if you ask me. Realistic too. He doesn't deny the trials, but there's hope beyond them. God knows. God will reward.

Just as we are different in our appearance and in our background and in our levels of maturity and chronological age, so we experience different tests. For all you know, the person living in your neighborhood is going through one of the deepest times of her or his life. That may be where *you* are today. Fires rage. This vile world is no friend to grace, which means you may be in the heat of it. You may have run right up against the toughest test you've experienced so far.

I hope these two words will not seem hollow or pious when I write them: *Take hope.* Take hope that this is not going on without God's awareness. The Lord God knows the way you take, and it's not without purpose. After the fiery trial, you, too, will come forth as gold. You are being refined by the test He's allowed, and you are being reshaped in the process—purified and humbled. Better times are coming. If not soon, and if not later on this earth, they will come when you stand before Him and He distributes the "gold, silver, and precious stones." It will then be worth it all. Many of Job's rewards came while he was still alive on planet Earth. Yours may await you in Glory. Either way, God knows. God always remembers. God will reward.

We never know ahead of time the plans God has for us. Job had no prior knowledge or warning. That morning dawned like every other morning. The night had passed like any other night. There was no great angelic manifestation—not even a tap on his window or a note left on the kitchen table.

In one calamity after another, all the buildings on his land are gone, and nothing but lumber and bodies litter the landscape. It occurred so fast, Job's mind swirled in disbelief. Everything hit broadside . . . his world instantly changed.

You and I *must* learn from this! We never know what a day will bring, good or ill. Our heavenly Father's plan unfolds apart from our awareness. Ours is a walk of faith, not sight. Trust, not touch. Leaning long and hard, not running away. No one knows ahead of time what the Father's plan includes. It's best that way. It may be a treasured blessing; it could be a test that drops us to our knees. He knows ahead of time, but He is not obligated to warn us about it or to remind us it's on the horizon. We can be certain of this: Our God knows what is best.

> *"FOR I KNOW THE PLANS THAT I HAVE FOR YOU," DECLARES THE LORD, "PLANS FOR WELFARE AND NOT FOR CALAMITY TO GIVE YOU A FUTURE AND A HOPE. THEN YOU WILL CALL UPON ME AND COME AND PRAY TO ME, AND I WILL LISTEN TO YOU. YOU WILL SEEK ME AND FIND ME WHEN YOU SEARCH FOR ME WITH ALL YOUR HEART."*
>
> Jeremiah 29:11–13

Here's a lesson worth remembering from Job: *A vertical perspective will keep us from horizontal panic.* Don't misunderstand Job's response to the devastation. Job didn't escape into some

mental state of denial. He faced the music—somber and sad that it was. He was so overwhelmed by all the loss he tore his robe. He was broken and saddened and grieved over the death of his kids. That's why he shaved his head and later sat in ashes. In fact, these reactions assure us he refused to escape emotionally through denial. But don't miss his ultimate response. He fell to the ground and worshiped.

His vertical perspective is clear and undaunting. Nothing that happens on the horizontal plane will cause this man to panic. It's as if Job is saying, "I had. I enjoyed. I was blessed. I'm now without those benefits. They're no longer a part of my world. I'm heartbroken over the loss of my family. But the same God who gave all of this by His grace, is the God who in His sovereign will has chosen to take each one away. I honor and praise Him. May His name be forever exalted!"

When life trucks along comfortably and contentedly, in good health and with a happy family . . . my, my! How high our view of God can be! How thrilled we are with all those wonderful verses of Scripture. How we hang on the words of the pastor's sermons. And how fervently we sing the songs of celebration. But let hardship arrive or let our health take a nosedive, how quickly our song is silenced, how cynical our attitude, how sour our faith becomes, and how quickly we're tempted to lower our view of God. The man is correct. It's easy to question God when hard times replace good times. A strong vertical perspective fans the flame of passion.

> "WE TAKE THE GOOD DAYS FROM GOD—WHY NOT ALSO THE BAD DAYS?"
>
> Job 2:10, MSG

What great theology! "God isn't our God only when times are good. Our faith in Him isn't limited to those days He blesses us. We don't claim Him as our Lord only when we get what we want. He's our God even when adversity strikes. He is Lord of good days and bad days. He didn't leave us the day I started suffering!" Job was right on. Talk about a passion!

Final Lessons

When trouble comes we have two options. We can view it as an intrusion, an outrage, or we can see it as an opportunity to respond in specific obedience to God's will. This is that rugged virtue James calls "endurance" (James 5:11).

Endurance is not jaw-clenched resignation, nor is it passive acquiescence. It is "a long obedience in the same direction." It is a dogged determination to pursue holiness when the conditions of holiness are not favorable. It is a choice in the midst of our suffering to do what God has asked us to do, whatever it is, and for as long He asks us to do it. As Oswald Chambers wrote, *"To choose suffering makes no sense at all; to choose God's will in the midst of our suffering makes all the sense in the world."*

Then Job answered the Lord and said,

"I KNOW THAT YOU CAN DO ALL THINGS."

Job 42:2

The first lesson Job teaches us: *There is nothing God cannot do.* Having heard and having realized the unlimited power of his infinite God, Job states his realization in the simplest of terms, "You can do all things." In other words, God is "omnipotent." The first part of that interesting word, omni means all. And of course, potent means powerful or effective. God is all-powerful. This affirms that He has no limitations, needs no approval, faces no obstacle that hinders His activities in any way. His actions run their course without resistance. The works of our heavenly Father are always and completely effective.

God's power is infinite and independent, self-energized, and never depleting. He creates from nothing without any decrease of energy. He sustains all life without needing any assistance. He gives life and takes life. He raises from the dead those He wishes to raise without any resistance. And He withholds the most powerful creature ever created (Satan himself) with no struggle, without restraint. Nothing stands in God's way. Nothing hinders God's work. Nothing alters God's plan. He alone deserves the description, "awesome."

AND THAT NO PURPOSE OF YOURS CAN BE THWARTED.

Job 42:2

What is the second lesson? *It is impossible to frustrate God's purposes.* In Job's words we find the term *thwarted.* God's priorities are never thwarted. The Hebrew term is from the verb that means "to cut off." "No purpose of Yours can be cut off." God's purpose can't be blocked, restrained, or stopped. God's intentions can neither be altered nor disrupted. What He purposes will transpire without delay, without hindrance, and without fail. Everything that happens on this earth falls within the framework of exactly what God has purposed. Yes, *exactly.* None of what occurs is a last-minute, stopgap response, therefore He is never surprised. Whatever occurs is unfolding precisely as He has planned it in His omniscience. With Him, things that occur on earth are never out of control.

Which brings us to a third lesson worth remembering: *God's plans are beyond our understanding and too deep to explain.*

> WHO IS THIS THAT HIDES COUNSEL WITHOUT
> KNOWLEDGE? THEREFORE I HAVE DECLARED THAT
> WHICH I DID NOT UNDERSTAND, THINGS TOO
> WONDERFUL FOR ME, WHICH I DID NOT KNOW.
>
> Job 42:3

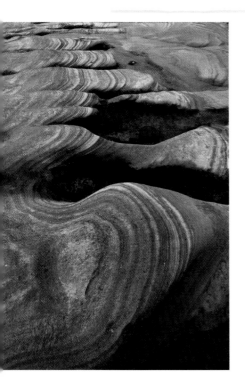

It took humility to say that.

If you were to ask me to give you the core message of the Book of Job, I'd have you read Job 42:3. Job's story is about coming to an understanding that God's plans are beyond our understanding and too deep to explain.

Do not be hesitant to admit that there are times we are downright *disappointed* with God. I mean, after all, we have done what is right, and we have done it for all the right reasons; yet look at what has transpired! How could He have permitted such a thing? Because God has revealed Himself as good and fair, compassionate and loving, we anticipate His responding in ways that fit His character (as we understand it). But, He doesn't "come through."

What bothers us is that He doesn't act like we think He *ought* to act. He doesn't do what our earthly dads would have done in similar circumstances. While I'm at it, where was He when His own Son was crucified? To the surprise of many (most?), He was there all the time working out His divine plan for our salvation. As the process was running its course, Jesus' own disciples didn't get it—they were the most disillusioned people on the planet. Do you remember what they were thinking? They were wondering how in the world they could have believed in a hoax. From their little-neck clam perspective, their Master's death didn't make any sense.

Do you know what Job finally sees? Job sees God and that is enough. He doesn't see answers. He is to the place where he doesn't *need* answers. He has gotten a glimpse of the Almighty and that is sufficient.

There is a fourth lesson worth remembering. *Only through God's instruction are we able to humble ourselves and rest in His will.*

HEAR, NOW, AND I WILL SPEAK;
I WILL ASK YOU AND YOU INSTRUCT ME.
I HAVE HEARD OF YOU BY THE HEARING OF THE EAR;
BUT NOW MY EYE SEES YOU;
THEREFORE I RETRACT,
AND I REPENT IN DUST AND ASHES.

Job 42:4–6

In gentle, resigned submission Job rests his case in the Father's will. He says, "You instruct me and as a result of Your instruction, I will willingly submit and accept it." Do you know what I love about Job's attitude? (Read this very carefully.) There is an absence of talk about "my rights." There is not a hint of personal entitlement. There is no expectation or demand. There's not even a plea for God to understand or to defend him before his argumentative friends. Furthermore, there's no self-pity, no moody, depressed spirit. He is completely at rest. His innermost being, at last, is at peace.

You may say, "Well, if God has blessed me like He blessed Job, I'd say that too." Wait. He hasn't yet brought relief or reward. The man is still covered with boils. He still doesn't have any family. He's still homeless. He's still bankrupt. With nothing external changed, Job says quietly, "Lord, I'm Yours."

We're ready for a fifth lesson: *When the day of reckoning arrives, God is always fair.* Do you remember another previous comment? All God's accounts are not settled at the end of the month. We've arrived at the place we've been waiting for. Let's call it the "Accounts Settlement" desk of God. Patiently and with long-suffering God has been observing everything, taking note of who is saying what. Not one idle word slips His attention. He not only knows what was said by whom, He knows why. He knows who spoke truth and who didn't. He deals with wrongdoers at His "Accounts Settlement" desk. He blesses those who have walked with Him. He forgives those who bring their offerings and humble themselves before Him. God restores. God rewards. God heals.

Closing Thoughts

I've never known anyone who deliberately set out to be heroic. You may have never thought of it, but the way you and I will be remembered by some who have watched us going through certain trials will be, from their perspective, an heroic accomplishment.

Travel back with me many centuries to a date the sands of time have now erased. To a place few could locate on a map. To a setting that seems almost idyllic. To a man who had no clue what extremes he would be called upon to endure. Even though this man was also a good husband and a devoted, faithful father, a businessman with great integrity, he would live to see all that change in a back-to-back sweep of devastating events. Interestingly, Job would be remembered—not for being healthy, wealthy, and wise—but for his heroic level of endurance after losing everything.

Centuries later, when another biblical character mentioned Job, he wrote "You have heard of the endurance of Job" (James 5:11). Using the Greek term, *hupomone*, James was saying, in effect, "You have heard of the man who stood fast, enduring under the load." Job's losses hit him like a two-ton pallet of bricks. Going through one blow after another, after another, after another, the man steadfastly endured. His name has become a byword for heroic endurance. Responding with the strength of character he had cultivated over years of trusting his God and walking with Him, the loss of everything did not cause Job to curse God and turn against Him. But it must have been terribly confusing.

Job died an old man and full of years. He truly came to know the living God, not in spite of his pain, but *because* of it. The pain drove him to his knees where he ultimately surrendered himself before his God. In complete trust, he rested in Him.

I invite you to trust Him right now in the midst of your circumstances. Let God be God. Remind yourself faithfully and regularly that you are not in charge. Limited, sinful, needy, and incapable of freeing yourself, I invite you to the Cross. That's where your burdens are rolled away and where God's music begins. Come to Him today. Let the music begin. It's a love song that invites you in.

Notes